11/07

History and Activities of
Ancient China

Jameson Anderson

Heinemann Library
Chicago, Illinois

Customer Service 888-454-2279
Visit our website at www.heinemannlibrary.com

Designed by Kimberly R. Miracle in collaboration with Cavedweller Studio
Originated by Chroma Graphics
Printed in China by WKT Company Limited

11 10 09 08 07
10 9 8 7 6 5 4 3 2 1

The Library of Congress has cataloged the first edition as follows:
Anderson, Jameson.
        History and activities of ancient China / Jameson Anderson.
            p. cm. -- (Hands-on ancient history)
            Audience: 4-6.
        Includes bibliographical references and index.
        ISBN 1-4034-7922-4 (HC) -- ISBN 1-4034-7930-5 (PB)
        1. China--Social life and customs--To 221 B.C.--Juvenile literature. I. Title.
        II. Series.

DS741.65.A53 2007
931--dc22   2005035163
13-digit ISBNs:
978-1-4034-7922-8 (hardcover)
978-1-4034-7930-3 (paperback)

Acknowledgments
The author and publishers are grateful to the following for permission to
reproduce photographs: AKG Photos, p. **10** (Erich Lessing); Alamy Images pp. **6**
(Panorama Stock Photos Co Ltd), **18** (Eddie Gerald); Ancient Art and Architecture
Collection, pp. **9** (R. Sheridan), **12** (Danita Delimont), **15**, **20** (R. Sheridan), **24**;
Art Archive, p. **13** (Topkapi Museum Istanbul/Dagli Orti); Art Directors and Trip,
p. **17** (Tibor Bognar); Art Resource, NY, p. **11** (Werner Forman); Bridgeman Art
Library, pp. **11**, **16**, **28**; Corbis, pp. **7** (Lowell Georgia), **8** (Jose Fuste Raga), **14**
(Asian Art and Archaeology Inc.); Harcourt, pp. **19** (David Rigg), **27** (David Rigg);

Cover photographs of Lao Tse astride a bull (foreground) reproduced
with permission of Art Resource, NY/ Snark and the Great Wall of China
(background) reproduced with permission of Corbis.

The publishers would like to thank May-lee Chai and Eric Utech for their
assistance in the preparation of this book.

Table of Contents

Some words are shown in bold, **like this.** You can find out what they mean by looking in the glossary.

Chapter 1: Nomads, Farmers, and Inventors

The Chinese civilization began more than 5,000 years ago. It is older than any other civilization. The ancient Chinese made many advances in science, arts, and learning. They invented things such as paper, math, and fireworks. Many of their inventions are still used today.

Dynasties

At first, the people of ancient China were **nomads**. They moved around a lot. They hunted animals and gathered berries. Later, people settled on farms. Kings and emperors ruled ancient China. They were organized into **dynasties**. Most dynasties were made up of powerful families. These families joined together with other families in the area. They agreed to help protect each other against enemies.

In 221 B.C.E. a man named Qin Shi Haungdi became the first emperor of China. His dynasty lasted until 207 B.C.E. The Han dynasty took over in 206 B.C.E. and lasted until C.E. 220. Other dynasties continued to rule China until 1912. China's civilization lasted for thousands of years. This makes it hard to decide where ancient China ends and modern China begins. This book covers the period from the Xia dynasty until about 100 B.C.E.

Timeline

1700–1500 B.C.E. Xia dynasty	**1500–1122 B.C.E.** Shang dynasty	**1040–221 B.C.E.** Zhou dynasty

551 B.C.E. Confucius is born.

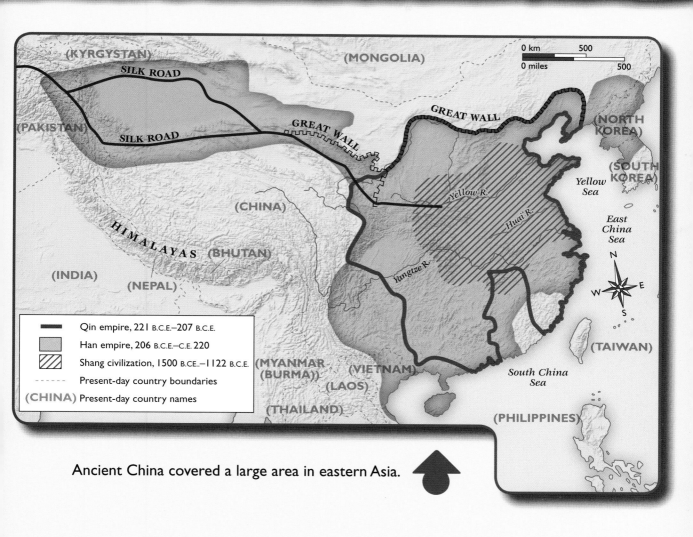

Ancient China covered a large area in eastern Asia.

221 B.C.E.–207 B.C.E.

Qin dynasty

105 B.C.E.

The Chinese invent silk.

100 B.C.E.

The Chinese invent paper.

"B.C.E." means "Before the Common Era," a time before Christianity was a popular religion. The term "B.C." is also used for this time period.

Xia dynasty

For years no one was certain that the Xia **dynasty** existed. There were Chinese myths and stories about the Xia, but no physical evidence. Then, in 1959, **archeologists** found artifacts from the Xia dynasty.

Historians now believe the Xia dynasty ruled China from 1700 to 1500 B.C.E. The Xia were farmers who used bronze weapons. They also made pottery. Xia rulers often acted as spiritual guides, as well as rulers. They regularly prayed to spirits for guidance.

Artifacts found in 1959 led to the discovery of the Xia dynasty.

The Shang and Zhou dynasties

Like the Xia, the Shang dynasty was once believed to be a myth. The Shang came into power in 1500 B.C.E. They are credited with inventing writing. Symbols that stood for words were carved into bones and shared between people of the dynasty. The Shang also carved symbols into turtle shells. Most of the writing was based on the group's spiritual beliefs.

Shang dynasty rulers were also religious leaders. The Shang believed that their kings could talk to the gods. They worshiped the Shang Di, a god who they believed controlled other gods such as the gods of the sun, moon, wind, and rain.

About 30 kings ruled throughout the Shang dynasty. When kings were buried, hundreds of their soldiers were killed and placed in burial tombs with them. The last king, Di Xin, did not care for his people. He took money from them and left them to fend for themselves.

A new dynasty began to emerge from the western borders of the Shang dynasty. The Zhou dynasty formed from **nomads** who were friendly to other people. As the Shang became angry with their leader Di Xin, the Zhou dynasty grew. The Zhou dynasty lasted from 1040–221 B.C.E.

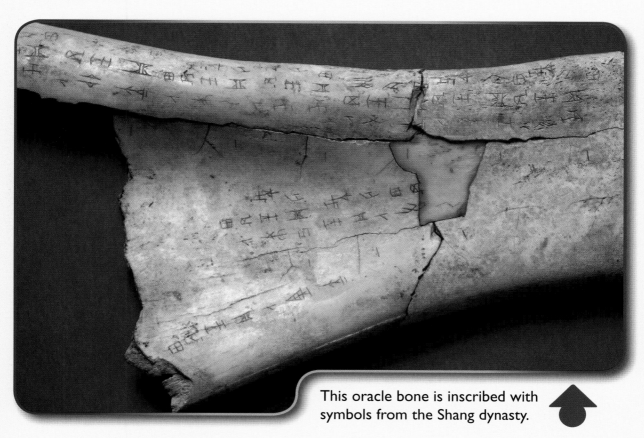

This oracle bone is inscribed with symbols from the Shang dynasty.

The last part of the Zhou dynasty (445–221 B.C.E.) is known as the "Warring Period" because of a series of wars between different Chinese states. Despite the wars, this was a great time for philosophers. Schools of thought such as Confucianism, Taoism, and Legalism emerged from this time. Some of the most memorable Chinese poetry was also written at this time.

In 221 B.C.E., the Qin, a dynasty located in the western part of China, became dominant. The Qin united the other states. For the first time China became a unified empire.

Great Wall of China

The Great Wall of China was originally built in small sections by groups of farmers who wanted to keep land to themselves. Early sections of the wall were made of stone.

As farmers expanded their land, and new emperors came into rule, the walls were rebuilt and extended. The Qin emperor ordered that the walls be connected to form one great wall that curves 4,161 miles (6,700 kilometers) from east to west across northern China. Along the wall are watchtowers where the emperors' men watched for enemies.

Today, visitors from around the world come to see the Great Wall of China.

Philosophy

Philosophers told people what the world means and how people should react to the world. Confucianism, Taoism, and Legalism were the main schools of **philosophy** to emerge from the Zhou dynasty.

In this art from ancient China, philosophers share lessons with young people.

Confucianism:
Confucius, born in 551 B.C.E., was a well-known scholar. He believed that everyone should be happy with where they are in life. Confucius said that everyone is born good and has a duty to take care of each other.

Taoism:
Tao means "the way." Taoists believe that everything in nature works together. That is "the way." Anyone who follows "the way," they believe, will live a harmonious life.

Legalism:
Legalists believed that the government could establish harsh rules and a stronger ethic code as an example for all people to follow.

Chapter 2: Life in Ancient China

Farm life

Many ancient Chinese were **nomads**. They moved from place to place to find animals to hunt and berries to pick. When animals moved or wild berries ran out, families had to move to where food was available.

Later, the Chinese began setting up farms. They changed from a nomadic to a more settled lifestyle. Most farms were run by extended families. Everyone in the family worked together. They grew wheat, rice, or millet. Most farming was done with hand tools. Some wealthy farmers could afford to use oxen plows.

Most families could live off their crops. However, emperors charged **taxes** to the farmers. A family who were unable to pay their taxes could be forced to work on another farm.

Farming was a way of life in ancient China. Most families supported themselves by raising crops.

Village markets

Some adults made crafts to sell at markets. Each village had a market where craft makers sold their products.

Silk was an important product. Silk makers sold and traded their product with other Chinese and with visitors from other lands. Silk was used to make clothes for nobles and wealthy people.

 People who lived in ancient Chinese cities often worked and traded in the markets.

 Women in ancient China made silk from the coccoons of silkworms.

How silk was made

Silk is made from moth larvae called silkworms. In ancient China, women kept silkworms to use their cocoons to form thread. Silk thread appears when a silkworm's cocoon is boiled. They wove this thread into cloth. A legend says that silk was discovered by accident when a cocoon fell into an emperor's wife's tea. When she pulled the cocoon from the hot water, silk thread was exposed.

Paper

Around 100 B.C.E. the Chinese invented paper. The first paper was very expensive. The paper was made of silk fibers squeezed together.

Soon paper could be made by mashing plants and rags with water and pressing them together. This made paper cheaper.

Paper was first used by nobles in the government. They already understood the written language. The nobles wrote messages from the emperor on paper and took them to villages. This meant that information could be read to peasants. The nobles who could read had more power than the peasants.

Homes

Housing in China changed a lot during ancient times. Early **nomads** lived in straw huts on the ground in the middle of the country.

Those in ancient China who understood the written language had the most power.

Later, the ancient Chinese built homes on farms and villages. Homes in villages were made of wood and bamboo. Fire could spread quickly from house to house. In cities, several families lived together in one large house. People slept on mats on the floor in southern China. In northern China they slept on platforms. Warm coals were put under the platforms to keep the sleeper warm in the winter.

Families built several buildings on farms. These buildings were used to store crops and hold animals.

Clothing

The people of ancient China wore mostly long, plain clothes known as tunics. The tunics were often made of fibers found in plants such as hemp. Men and women both wore pants under their tunics.

Nobles in ancient China wore fancier clothes. They wore long, silk robes. The robes were decorated with inks and dyes made from plants. Sometimes patterns were painted on to the robes, other times they were sewn into the fabric.

Nobles in ancient China wore brightly colored clothing.

Dancing

Street performers entertained the crowds in villages in ancient China. Musicians, dancers, and acrobats entertained people in the cities. They also performed for emperors and nobility.

Dancing was very popular. Young girls danced on top of round balls. They wore bright colored costumes. They often twirled ribbons while they danced. The ancient Chinese played bells and chimes. These made music for the girls to dance to.

Dancing occurred during festivals. Dancing was also used to celebrate the New Year or the emperor's birthday. Many religious ceremonies involved dancing. Groups of dancers toured from village to village to perform.

This sculpture shows the importance of dancing in ancient China.

Music in ancient China was considered spiritual.

Music

There was always music with dancing. Music was taken more seriously than dancing in ancient China. The ancient Chinese believed that music had special powers. Some people thought that music could affect a person's behavior. Some music could make people do good things. Other music could make people do bad things.

The most common musical instruments in ancient China were bronze bells. Other instruments included drums, chimes, and flutes.

Sports

Children and adults both played sports. The ancient Chinese often played a game similar to football. Noble men and women also played a version of polo. Like modernday polo, the game was played on horseback. Players decorated their horses' tails with ornaments. Leaders used the game to get to know each other. The Chinese versions of football and polo were both used as training exercises for the Chinese military.

The most common sport was hunting. It was a very exciting sport. It was also a useful way of catching food. The ancient Chinese hunted with trained falcons. Nobility and peasants both hunted for rabbits and pheasants.

 Horses such as the one shown in this sculpture were used to play a form of polo.

 The ancient Chinese enjoyed playing board games.

Games

The ancient Chinese played board games and card games. Some games were very similar to ones that are played today. Games were played on holidays such as the New Year or the emperor's birthday.

Many games and sports in ancient China started during other activities. Hunters practiced throwing spears and knives. This practice sometimes turned into a competition.

Other sports grew out of army training. Emperors always wanted their armies to be stronger. They ordered warriors to fight against each other. Crowds gathered when the warriors fought. The wrestling between warriors became a form of entertainment.

Warriors also competed in horse races and stone throwing contests.

By doing the hands-on activities and crafts in this chapter, you'll get a feel for what life was like for people who lived and worked in ancient China.

Warning!

Always make sure an adult is present when using a hot oven.

Make sure to read all directions before starting the recipe.

Recipe: Moon Cakes

The ancient Chinese celebrated the changing of the seasons. Harvest moon, or mid-autumn, festivals have been celebrated in ancient China since the Tang dynasty. The festival celebrates the brightest moon of the year. Today, Chinese families prepare foods such as moon cakes to celebrate the new moon.

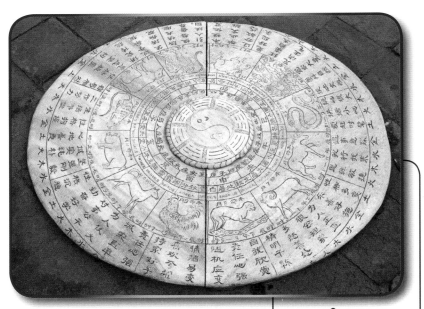

Ancient Chinese stones like this one show calendar markings.

Ingredients and supplies

- Homemade dough or tube of "ready to use" dough
- Rolling pin
- 1 small jar of grape jam or bean paste
- round cookie cutter or small juice glass
- cookie sheet
- spatula

1. Roll out dough to 1/4-inch thickness. Cut into circles with a cookie cutter.

2. Place the circles on a cookie sheet.

3. Prick the circles with a fork to prevent puffing while cooking.

4. Bake the circles at 350 °F (180 °C, gas mark 4) until slightly puffed, light golden brown, and cooked through.

5. Remove the cookie sheet from the oven and let cool.

6. With a spatula, move the moon cakes to a plate.

7. Spread jam or bean paste on one moon cake and top it with another moon cake.

Moon Cakes

Moon cakes can be eaten as part of a celebration.

Craft: Make an Abacus

It is hard to imagine counting without numbers, but there was a time when written numbers did not exist. An abacus helped shopkeepers and other people keep track of large numbers. Many cultures used abacuses, but the abacus we are most familiar with today was invented by the Chinese.

Supplies
- 6 craft sticks
- 3 additional craft sticks (optional)
- 56 plastic "pony beads"
- 3 1/8" diameter dowel rods (available at hardware stores) each approximately 12 inches long
- Pencil
- School glue

The ancient Chinese used an abacus to do math.

1. Have an adult help you break your dowel rods into thirds. It is possible to cut the dowel rods with strong classroom scissors. Or, have an adult score them with a knife where you want the cuts to be, and carefully break the dowel rod on the scores.

2. Place a craft stick on your work surface. Place the ends of eight dowel rods along the craft stick, equally spaced. Mark their places with a pencil and remove the dowel rods. (See Picture A)

A

3. Carefully squeeze glue onto your pencil lines. Reposition the dowel rod ends into the glue. Let the glue dry.

4. After the glue dries, thread two pony beads onto each dowel rod. These are the "heaven beads." Each "heaven bead" represents a unit of five.

5. Place a second craft stick underneath the dowel rods. Leave some room between this stick and the beads so that you have room to move the beads back and forth between the craft sticks. This new stick will separate the "heaven beads" from the "earth beads" in step 7. (See Picture B)

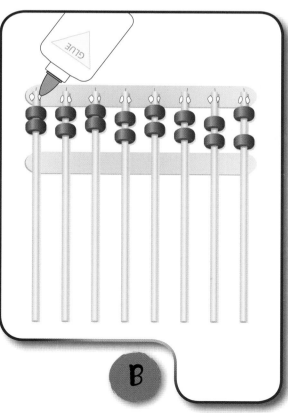

B

6 Mark the positions of the dowel rods on the second craft stick with a pencil. Just like before, glue the dowel rods to the craft stick on these lines. Do not accidentally glue the beads so that they cannot move!

7 After the glue has dried, thread five pony beads onto each dowel rod. These are the "earth beads." Each "earth bead" represents a unit of one. (See Picture C)

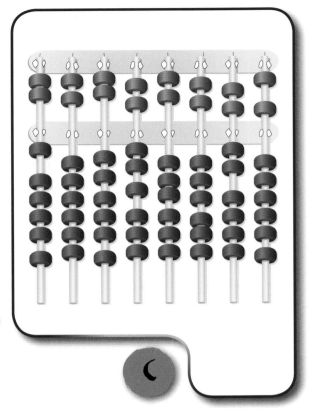

C

8 Place a third craft stick under the tips of the dowel rods. Just like before, mark their positions with a pencil, and glue the dowel rods in place.

9 While the glue is drying, place another craft stick over your first craft stick and sandwich the dowel rods in between. Make sure the two craft sticks are lined up, then carefully glue the new stick down to the dowel rods. (See Picture D)

10 Repeat this process on the second and third craft sticks, gluing new craft sticks to the dowel rods so that they are sandwiched between the craft sticks.

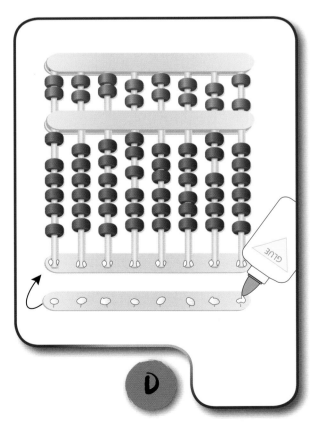

D

11 If you want to be able to move the beads more easily, glue additional craft sticks to the bottom side of your abacus so that the beads are suspended above the work surface.

⬆ Abacus

You can use your finished abacus to help solve math problems.

How do you think you use an abacus to do math? After coming up with your own theory, consider looking online, or in a reference book for the answer.

Craft: Make Paper

The ancient Chinese invented paper and made it by pressing tree bark and cloth rags together. You can make your own paper out of old newspapers.

Warning!

This is a messy project; protect your clothes and work surface. Have an adult use the blender.

Read all the directions before beginning the project.

In ancient China, paper was made from tree bark and cloth rags.

A note on supplies:

This project requires a papermaking screen. The easiest way to make one of these is to use an old screen and frame from a small window. A screen can also be made by placing flexible nylon screening over the inside part of an embroidery hoop. Then attach the outer hoop, with the screen side up. You can also staple flexible screening to an old picture frame to make your own permanent papermaking screen.

This project is a great opportunity to use leftover scraps of construction paper from other projects. Or use paper towels, tissue paper, or newspaper—but not shiny paper or office paper.

Supplies:
- Papermaking screen
- Assorted recyclable paper
- Electric blender
- Plastic bin large enough to hold the papermaking screen.
- Kitchen towels or recyclable newspapers or paper towels
- Spatula
- Rolling pin
- Cookie sheet (optional)
- Liquid starch (optional)
- Glitter, confetti, or dried flowers (optional)
- Hairdryer (optional)

1 Tear the scraps of paper into pieces about the size of postage stamps. Keep in mind that if you mix colors of paper it will be like mixing colors of paint, so choose which colors you mix carefully.

2 Pour 1 cup of warm water into the blender. Place scraps of paper into the blender loosely until they are almost to the top of the blender. Do not pack down the paper!

3 With the lid on, have an adult turn the blender on at its lowest setting. If there appears to be too much paper, turn the blender off, add a little more water, and try again. If you still need more water, have the adult continue to add water until the blender turns. The mixture should be the consistency of applesauce. This process separates the wood fibers. Papermakers call this mixture pulp. If you are going to write on this paper, have an adult mix 2 teaspoons of starch into this mixture.

4 Fold the kitchen towels, paper towels, or newspapers into a pad about one inch thick and about the same size as your screen. This pad, called a couching mound, goes on your work surface. Place a cookie sheet under it if you need to keep the work surface dry.

5 Place the screen into the plastic bin, flat on the bottom. Make sure the screen side of the frame is facing up. (See Picture A)

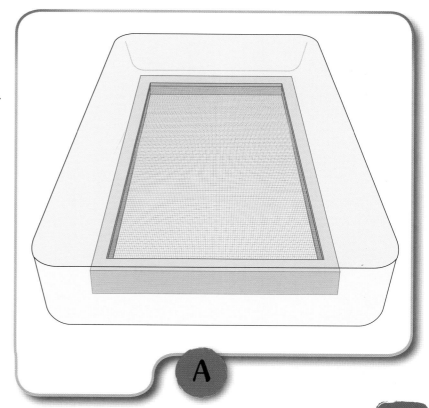

A

6 Carefully pour the pulp from the blender onto the screen. Try to cover the screen evenly. If you see a lot of holes in your paper, pour the pulp back into the blender, and add more paper. Keep mixing in enough paper so that the pulp is thick enough to stick to the surface of the screen.

7 When the pulp has had a minute or two to drain on the screen, carefully move the screen to the couching mound.

8 In one quick motion, turn the screen over onto the couching mound. Carefully and slowly rock the screen from one edge to the other to loosen the paper onto the couching mound. You can also use a spatula to separate the paper from the screen. (See Picture B)

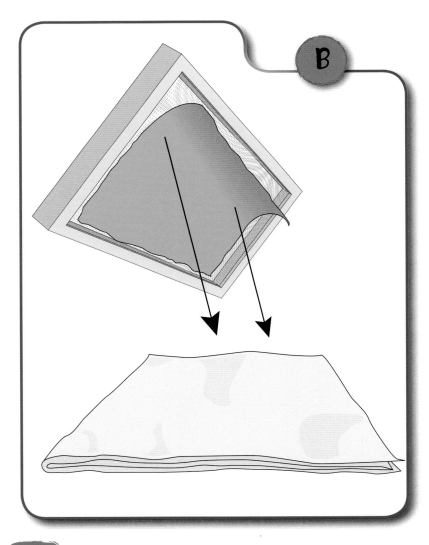

B

9 Place a towel or layer of paper towels over your paper sheet. Use a rolling pin to carefully press out more water. Gently remove the top towel, and move your new paper to a place to dry. If it looks like it will rip, leave it on the topmost towel of your couching mound and move it, towel and paper, to a sunny location or use a hairdryer to dry it more quickly.

10 Finished sheets can be hung on a clothesline to dry some more.

⓫ Once you have learned the process, try adding different materials to your pulp, such as glitter.

Homemade Paper

Your finished project can now be used to make a card for a parent or friend.

Cotton fibers, cardboard egg carton pieces, shredded comic pages, confetti, dried flowers, or glitter could be added to the pulp or to the surface of the damp sheet before it dries. What will adding these materials do to your paper?

Activity: Do The Tiger Walk

Many Chinese exercises imitate the movements of animals. The ancient Chinese respected the tiger. According to the Chinese calendar, those born in the year of the tiger are sensitive and short-tempered.

The purpose of the tiger walk exercise is to develop flexibility in your spine and hips.

The tiger was a respected animal in ancient China.

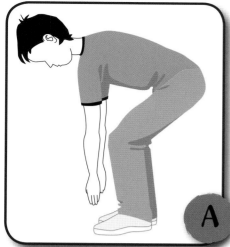

1. Stand with your feet separated at shoulder width.

2. Bend your trunk forward, and bend your knees so that your back is almost parallel with the floor. (See Picture A)

3. Grab your left ankle with your left hand, and your right ankle with your right hand. (See Picture B)

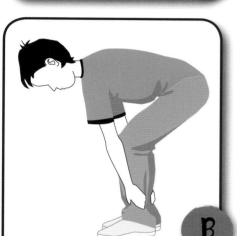

4. Take a step forward with the right foot, while turning your head to the right. (See Picture C)

5. Take a step forward with your left foot, while turning your head to the left.

6. Walk eight steps in this manner.

7. Release ankles and return to standing position.

8. Repeat exercise two to four times.

As you were doing the tiger walk, you were low to the ground like a tiger. Did you see the room as a tiger might see it?

Glossary

archeologist person who studies the remains of past cultures

dynasty families who rule an area for more than one generation

nomad person who moves around from place to place following a food supply

philosophy way of thinking about the world

tax fee paid to a ruler or government

More Books To Read

Deady, Kathleen W. and Muriel L. Dubois, *Ancient China*. Mankato, Minn: Capstone Press, 2003.

Minnis, Ivan. *You Are in Ancient China*. Chicago: Raintree, 2005.

Rees, Rosemary. *The Ancient Chinese*. Chicago: Heinemann Library, 2002.

A Note to Teachers

The instructions for these projects are designed to allow students to work as independently as possible. However, it is always a good idea to make a prototype before assigning any project so that students can see how their own work will look when completed. Prior to introducing these projects, teachers should collect and prepare the materials and be ready for any modifications that may be necessary. Participating in the project-making process will help teachers understand the directions and be ready to assist students with difficult steps. Teachers might also choose to adapt or modify the projects to better suit the needs of an individual student or class. No one knows what levels of achievement students will reach better than their teacher.

While it is preferable for students to work as independently as possible, there is some flexibility in regards to project materials and tools. They can vary according to what is available. For instance, while standard white glue may be most familiar to students, there might be times when a teacher will choose to simplify a project

by using a hot glue gun to fasten materials for students. Likewise, while a project may call for leather cord, it is feasible in most instances to substitute vinyl cord or even yarn or rope. In another instance, acrylic paint may be recommended because it adheres better to a material like felt or plastic, but other types of paint would be suitable as well. The materials and tools that one uses can vary according to what is available. For example, circles can be drawn with a compass, or simply by tracing a cup, roll of tape, or other circular object. Allowing students a broad spectrum of creativity and opportunities to problem-solve within the parameters of a given project will encourage their critical thinking skills most fully.

Each project contains an italicized question somewhere in the directions. These questions are meant to be thought-provoking and promote discussion while students work on the project.

Index